Translations

David Wevill

Translations

Shearsman Books

Published in the United Kingdom in 2022 by
Shearsman Books
P O Box 4239
Swindon
SN3 9FN

Shearsman Books Ltd Registered Office
30–31 St. James Place, Mangotsfield, Bristol BS16 9JB
(this address not for correspondence)

www.shearsman.com

ISBN 978-1-84861-833-6

ACKNOWLEDGMENTS

The Pessoa translations and six of the Lacerda translations were first
collected in David Wevill's *Figure of Eight: New Poems and Selected
Translations* (Toronto: Exile Editions, 1987). These were republished
with the additional Lacerda poems featured here, with the Pindar
translations and with a large selection of poems by Ferenc Juhász, in
David Wevill, *Collected Translations* (Portland, OR: Tavern Books,
2014). The Juhász poems will republished by Shearsman Books
as a separate volume.

Contents

Pindar

Translations

CHARLES BAUDELAIRE

Charles Baudelaire (1821–1867) was one of the founding spirits of modernism, and a leading French symbolist poet. He introduced Edgar Allan Poe's work to Europe. His poetry, prose pieces and critical essays have had a lasting influence on European literature. He published one book of poems, *Les Fleurs du Mal,* which remains a classic. His poems, traditional in form, are revolutionary in content, exploring, with striking imagery, the world of the unconscious in all its beauty and perversity, a sensuous world where all the senses come together in a dance of emotion and imagination. His sonnet 'The Owls', printed here, is my stripped-down version of his elegantly formal original.

The Owls

Beneath the black yews that hide them

the owls take up their stations.
Their eyes flash red. Like strange
visitor gods, they meditate.

Nothing moves. They wait there
until, the flattened sun now
pushed under by shadows,
the dark takes over.

From their posture, the wise learn
to shy clear of this world's
turbulence & restlessness –

men, maddened by shadows that pass
bearing always the punishment
of wanting some place else.

FERNANDO PESSOA

These Pessoa translations are the work of Alberto de Lacerda and myself equally, and appeared originally under both our names. A native of Portugal, Fernando Pessoa (1888–1935) claimed that Álvaro de Campos, Alberto Caeiro, and Ricardo Reis were not pseudonyms but deep, uncontrollable expressions of his personalities, or *heterónimos* [heteronyms] as he called them. The names of the presiding *heterónimos* have been noted at the bottom of each of the Pessoa poems in this volume.

After the Fair

They wander down the road
Singing for no reason,
A final gift: of hope
For the ultimate illusion.
They don't mean anything.
They are only fools and mimes.

They go, together and
Singly through the moonlight,
Lost in some dream
They will never know,
Singing the words of these poems
That come to mind.

Pages from some dead myth,
So lyrical, so lonely!
No cry breaks their voices,
The voices are scarcely their own.
And the infinite has never
Heard of them, or of us.

Fernando Pessoa

[Every Day I Discover]

Every day I discover
The incredible reality of things.
Each thing is what it is,
Intact; and it's hard to explain to someone how much
This delights and fills me.
To exist is enough to be whole.

I have written so many poems.
Of course I shall write many more.
Every poem of mine says this,
And none of my poems is the same,
Since everything that exists is another way of saying it.

Sometimes I'll look at a stone.
I am not concerned whether a stone can feel.
The stone is not my sister –
I like it because it is a stone,
Because it feels nothing
And is no relation of mine.

Other times I hear the wind passing.
I think it is worth being born, to hear the passing wind.

I don't know what the world will make of this.
But I feel it is true, because thinking this way
Is my nature; and no one

Can hear me thinking.
My thoughts live only in words.

Once I was called a
"Materialist poet" – surprised
That my soul had a name.
I am no poet, I just have eyes.
If my words matter, the matter is there
In my poems, not in me. My will
Is no part of my poems. They exist.

Alberto Caeiro

Henry the Navigator

On his throne among the shining spheres,
In his cloak of night and solitude,
At his feet the new ocean, and the past ages –
He is the one emperor
Who truly holds the world's globe in his hand.

Fernando Pessoa

Ode

To be great you must be whole. Don't
Exaggerate or leave things out.
Be whole in everything, put your whole
Self into the smallest thing you do.
So the full moon, from her height,
Shines over every lake.

Ricardo Reis

On a Book Abandoned on a Journey

I came from near Beja.
I am going straight into Lisbon
bringing nothing with me: and I shall find nothing.
I am weary with what I shall not find,
and the longing I feel is neither for present nor future.
I record, here, this image of myself:
I existed, like grass, and I was not uprooted.

Álvaro de Campos

SAN JUAN DE LA CRUZ

The life and artistic accomplishment of Spanish poet and mystic San Juan de la Cruz (1542–1591) is too vast to do justice to in this briefest of introductions. The Baroque Renaissance Spanish of San Juan de la Cruz is impossible to capture in anything like readable, modern English. I feel that my translation of 'The Dark Night' is a quieter, more lyrical version than the typical representations of this great poem.

The Dark Night

On a dark night
love's anguish burning in me
O blessed risk
I went out, no one saw me
the house now quiet and still

Safely in the dark
by the secret ladder, disguised
O blessed chance
hidden in the dark
my house now quiet and still

In the night blest with secrecy
for no one saw me
and my self saw nothing
led by no other light
but what burned in my heart to guide me

which led me on
more surely than the light of noon
to where someone waited
whom I knew intimately
in a place where no one came

O night that led me on
night more obliging than any dawn
O night bringing together
the lover and the loved one
the beloved transformed in the Lover

On my flowering breast
kept only and wholly for him
he lay sleeping
while I caressed him
fanned by breezes from the cedar trees

A breeze off the parapets,
then as I spread out his hair
with a hand light as air
he touched and hurt my neck,
and all my senses hung there

I stayed, I forgot myself
I laid my face against my Lover
Everything stopped, my self
my cares behind me
among the lilies forgotten

ALBERTO DE LACERDA

Born in Mozambique, Alberto de Lacerda (1928–2007) was one of Portugal's most distinguished and admired poets. During his lifetime, de Lacerda worked as an announcer for the BBC, freelance journalist, teacher (both at the University of Texas at Austin and Boston University), critic, and translator. My versions of Alberto de Lacerda's poems were done with his help and guidance, though the responsibility for the final versions is mine alone.

Four

Man and geometry
the light
and the sword

man
and geometry
the light and the sword

man

    geometry

        light

           sword

man and light
geometry
and the sword

light
and man
geometry   and the sword

(man) light
(man) sword

the gods

Yucatán—Mexico
28 Dec. '69

[Bones of Man]

Bones of man
Bones of woman

The pyramid stairs prolong
 its subterranean flight

down
to the dark-

most galleries
of the blood

Mérida—Yucatán
29 Dec. '69

In Hadrian's Palace

This is a temple of absolute love
whole, like marble or water
that do not hesitate, make no mistakes

This is the palace of a love born
ancient, limitless, without question or
answer. Oneself's gift:, everything,
soul: meeting herself at the knife-
edge, where the horizon overflows

This is the palace of Hadrian
the temple of Antinous
the palace of love, tender, love, child,
adult, and so deepened, death
suddenly gave it back
to be immortal

Villa Adriana—Italy
10 Aug. '69

Poem for Octavio Paz

Where the conjunction is
                            disjointed
mutilated snake
of time

eating its own tail

Mérida—Yucatán
31 Dec. '69

[Here]

Here

time
exists

stone
phallus, visible

from all four corners of

creation

Mérida—Yucatán
31 Dec. '69

Palace of Piero della Francesca

I

This place is sacred. Grace, here
unfolding image, stone
apparitions on skin of water. Fish
multiplied nameless dance
Queen of Sheba
                    Throne
                                A naked
boy, his back turned

blue light, and the silence white
news of another sea and depth
where dance, motionless, innocent
incarnate presence

II

This place, is sacred. Grace here
unfolding, image, fish
apparitions on skin of stone. Fish
multiplied nameless dance
stone, fish, stone, faceted,
thrones
            battles

columns

dividing

not tragic, the light, indivisible, light

Arezzo—Italy
16 Aug. '69

[Your Beauty Hurts]

Your beauty hurts
                    silence beyond
that open door

Austin—Texas
2 Oct. '69

Ceremony

Dance is the gesture
In which man touches
The palm of the hand of the god

New Mexico
22 Mar. '70

[Sun Within]

Sun within
sun without

internal sun bestowing
external sun bestowing demanding

snake
uncoiling towards the sun

the root colours
resolved in the pillar of sun

sun
in majesty

Mexico City
21 Dec. '69

PINDAR

Pindar (Pindaros) (518–432 BC or 522–438 BC). Born near Thebes. About a fourth of his works survive, chiefly Odes, commissioned to celebrate victors in the Olympian, Pythian, Nemean, and Isthmian games. 'They were meant to be sung by a chorus. The Odes combine grandeur of voice, bold and elaborate imagery, and retell and weave together classical myths and themes, usually connected with the place of origin of the victors. Pindar is one of the most admired poets of the classical age. These versions are much freer in form than the originals, and were done with the essential collaboration of Donald Carne-Ross, who provided the literals, extensive notes, and much encouragement throughout.

Pythian 3

If Khiron were alive
If Khiron were

           but he's dead
the great centaur
whose spirit walked the wooded hill

wild creature
whose heart was human
               who taught
Asklepios how to cure
man's illness of mind and body

that great healer, whose mother
Koronis
       not yet nine months gone with child
was pierced by the arrows of Artemis

and sank
in a dream
into Hades –

it was Apollo's doing,
the gods do not play at anger
               but she
stupidity!

mocked the will of a god
said "yes" to another man
                having slept with Apollo
caressed his fine hair…

                        Koronis
his seed in your body
and you, unwilling to wait
for the marriage rites
                Apollo's consent, and your father's
the songs
the young girls sing
at evening, under your window

Her desire, common enough
for what she did not have

                like a man
whose eyes
wandering the horizon
trips over stones

hunting for ghosts in the wind

You were blind, Koronis
beauty no help to you, stubborn

from Arkadia came a stranger –
did his bed warm you more than Apollo's fire?

but Apollo
missing nothing

his mind like an intelligent wind
                          combing the earth, no
grain of sand can hide from

saw
how Koronis had tricked him

sent
Artemis to Thessaly armed with

arrows of fire
to the lake and cliff where she lived –

plague
took her,
many others

on high ground
one spark can eat a forest

But as she lay in the flames
and the fire-god danced on her body

Apollo cried
"Stop!

my child will not burn with his mother"
                        and plucked
the babe
from the glowing coal of her womb
                parting the fire like fronds

and straight to the mountain
to Khiron

Asklepios
his child in his arms

                "Great master
teach my son to heal the sick"

They came to him
with open sores

eczema, nerves
weeping through skin

spear wounds,
cuts from flying stones

summer fevers
winter fevers

and he healed them, cured
each of his own disease

murmuring spells for the mind-sick
draughts and herbs for the sick in body

bandaged wounds, put
poultices on ulcered limbs

and with his scalpel
taught others to walk again

But in the end, profit proved stronger than
wisdom. They paid him well, to raise a man up
from the dead, to perform the act of resurrection,
never before done by man … and Zeus

punished them both

        lightning
flared from his hand

death
burnt them to cinder

                We must not ask
the gods
for more than we are, mortals

knowing our path, our fate
                our human condition

Heart, do not ask
for immortal life

be what you are, beat
with the energy you were born with

on earth. If Khiron were still alive
in his cave
                    and my words had the power of a spell or
prayer on him

I would ask him to send
another healer
                    Asklepios
                                        or even Apollo
and take a ship, and sail the Ionian sea
to Syrakusa
                    where my host
the king
rules over his people
                    both noble and common
at peace
under the prowling storms of Etna

And if I had come
bringing two gifts –

health,
gold as the sun

and silver, the song that moistens the garlands
brought from Delphi
                    where Winner, his horse
ran first –

I would have shone in his eyes
brighter than the sky's most brilliant star

But all I can do
is pray
to Rhea, the great mother

whose singers come to my door at night
                    and Pan is with her
pray
to make you well

Do you know what the myths tell us
Hieron,
the old tales?
one good / two evils
        our lot
                in the eyes of the gods

fools
cannot accept this

great men can, and make the best of their fate

You have your share of fortune
A great king lives in the eye of
fate
    under the hawk's gaze –

Peleus –
Khiron helped him to win
a goddess for bride –

                he had his trials
and Kadmos
almost a god –
he suffered too

            And yet men say
these two had happier lives than most men
dream of,

        heard the muses
singing in the hills

              and in Thebes

Kadmos was married
and Peleus

        to Thetis, child of the sea-god

at the wedding feast
the gods ate at their tables

they received their gifts surrounded by gods
on their golden thrones

blest by Zeus
they outgrew their sorrows

hearts
beat like strong wings

But time
turned on Kadmos,
grief for his lost daughters
              though one
Semele
slept with Zeus
          gave birth to Dionysos

And Peleus, his only son
Akhilles
          lost to an arrow
his body blackening in the fire
              dirge of the Greek armies
drifting away in smoke

Knowing the way of truth
a man accepts what he's given
              his life feels lighter

now here
          now there
the high winds blow over the earth
              and a man

burdened by happiness
              is sure to lose it

When the moment is small, I will make myself small

when great, I will grow with it

trusting what fortune I have
using what gifts I have

If the gods offer a man wealth
and the luxury money brings with it

fame will be his
in the future –

Nestor,
Sarpedon –

Their story lives in our minds,
Homer has told it

A great poem gives life to a great act

Few can earn that poem

Pythian 9

For Telesikrates, who won the Pythian race
in shield and armour
                         Graces
this victory ode

for the runner bringing his garlands home to
                         Kyrene, city of chariot wheels
she

who long ago
in the green time of the gods
was a girl the passionate sun Apollo carried away

to a land of orchards far across the sea
cropped by sheep, green to the sea horizons

to flower in that soil
                    a queen
hers with the earth's root
                         her life and home

When Apollo's horses thundered out of the sun
Aphrodite was waiting

While his chariot cooled
she stroked its wheels
with her long delicate fingernails

and left a ghost of her musk in the bed where they
                              slept, for the first time
the god and Kyrene
                    child of Hypseus, king of the fierce
                    lapith hordes, a hero

He was born in the valleys of Pindos
both Earth and Ocean in his blood

A river god was his father
The nymph Kreousa his mother
                              was Earth's daughter

Raised by her father, Kyrene was no
debutante
       The loom bored her, the endless shuttle and

weave, and the prattle and small talk
of interminable dinners with

"suitable friends"

She was different
Her poise was the spear –

expert at tracking and killing
She'd get up at dawn, combing the woods and fields

by first light, when sleep
a girl's best friend is most seductive

Her father's cattle slept sweet as grass through her skill

So Apollo, ranging with the sun one morning
found her
            naked, alone, no spear
tackling a full-grown lion

                        Kheiron
meditating in his nearby cave
heard the god's voice calling
                            "Centaur –

leave your holy of holies for
one moment
                See how a mere girl
with enough nerve can twist a lion's tail!

Courage and sinews like hers most men would
kill to possess

her mind
cool as an upland frost
but no winter of fear can touch her heart

Tell me, who was her father?

For the hills roll and sway as her body moves
her courage reflects the sun

Am I permitted to grace her with my touch?
Reap the virgin grass of a bed like hers?"

        And Kheiron, the wise teacher
doctor, hunter, musician and prophet
answered –

        "Apollo
subtlety works
where skeleton keys fail

In love, gods are like men
they hate to have their beds invaded by eyes

Apollo, what can I tell you?
For you, lord, all knowledge is old as creation

You know the fate of all things
how the wheel turns from birth to death and returns

in the eternal round
of matter, dead and living

how many leaves there are in the spring
and grains of sand in the seas and rivers
                              driven by wind and water

past, present and future –
your eye reflects all

                              And you ask

who her father was?
Whether the girl is for you?

Then listen
		You come as a husband
to take her far across the sea
to the garden of Zeus

			She will be queen
of a city, a hill dividing a wide plain
and the island people will cluster like bees
				to their queen

And Libya
		queen of all the meadowland
will welcome your bride like a sister
in her villa baked by sunlight white as bone

granting her
land by deed of gift, immediately
the crops hers, the orchards in perpetuity

the power over wild creatures
			and all that breathes

She will give birth to a son
                    Hermes himself
will take the babe
to be cradled in the arms of Earth and the Hours

                    a prodigy
so great a destiny crying in their hands
they will wet his lips with
                    nectar and ambrosia

He will take the names of Zeus and Apollo
                    he will not die as mortals do
and men will pray to him
to guard their herds and make their pastures fertile

Aristaios
          protector of olives and vines
hunter and herdsman
                    lord of the bees
your son"

Gods when they move waste no time
One day was enough for Apollo

They galloped to Africa with the sun
and in the white light of the sun's corona
                              the bride-chamber
Apollo took her –

two bodies, all day long
burning in one flame

                    And now Telesikrates
returns with his garlands from Delphi

And she wakes again in the arms of her lover
Kyrene
        welcoming him home
home to his land of lovely women

he, and the prize he brings her back from Delphi

Acts that reflect the gods
are never forgotten
                    Myths multiply

The skill is to pick out a few bright threads
keep the tale short
            the whole in exact proportion

Think of Iolaos
when he cut off Eurystheus' head
and the Thebans buried him alive in the tomb of his father's

father
        Amphitryon
who had come to Thebes as a guest
of the race sown from the dragon's teeth

the Thebans   who ride white horses

It was his wife Alkmene
who bore him strong twin sons
                    Zeus had a part in it too

No man with half a mind
would forget to honour Herakles
                    or the name of the nursing spring
that fed him and his brother Iphikles

I owe them this debt at least a victory song
for deeds done
                    Graces
your pure light pluck my strings

At Aegina, I swear
and three times by the hill of Megara
                    praised the city of Thebes

escaping the white asylum walls of silence

"Praise where praise is due"
                    said the old man of the sea

Whether a man is friend or enemy
honor his finest deeds
done for the common good

When the women saw you win
year after year
                    in the games of Pallas Athene

each, in the dark of her soul
yearned for you
                    as a son or a lover

Telesikrates

there

       and in the Olympian games

            and the games for Gaia, the earth

But before I end my song
I owe a debt to your family, Telesikrates

so their name shines
with the light of a further star

I'd tell how they went to Libya
to Irasa

       to court the king's daughter
a beauty

       her hair a wave of chestnut flame

So many princes, cousins and strangers
begged for her hand

            the musk of her youth

drew them like boys to an orchard

But the king swore she could do better than princes

He remembered how Danaos, an Argive lord
had 48 daughters
                        and gave them away
in one race

where the girls stood in a long line
at the winning post
                        and the men ran

like cheetahs to catch the girl their speed deserved

So the Libyan king gave his daughter away
in a bride-race
                    planted her
at the winning post
                        perfect flower
to be plucked by the fastest runner

And it was
            Alexidamos
his long stride melting him through the runners
who touched her
                took her hand

and led her, grave and proud
through the crowd of nomad horsemen

and the air shakes like a tree full of doves' wings
as the leaves of his triumphs
                            so many
                                come flocking home

Olympian 6

For Hagesias of Syracuse,
whose mule-team won first
prize at Olympia

Gold pillars lifting the portico wings!

I would build a great house
that dazzles the eye

new work begun
must glow with the fire of the sun

if a man won the prize at Olympia
and prophesied at the sacred altar of Zeus

and came of the founding line
of Syracuse
                    her citizens
not grudging him
this ode –

how many praise-poems in his name!

Hagesias
this sandal fits your foot

risking nothing
no athlete born
            can be great
in men's eyes
or at sea on the curling hulls

but many remember
a feat of strength or skill
                Hagesias

fair praise for you
that the man who led the seven at Thebes
                    gave to another prophet
when earth
swallowed him down

his white horses melting under like snow

In Thebes
when the funeral pyres had died to ash
the leader said
                "I mourn him
eye of my army
great prophet
                       quick with a spear"

which is true
of this man from Syracuse
                       my song honours

I would quarrel with none
but swear this as an oath before the gods
                       for Hagesias

the muses' honey voices on my tongue

Phintis, yoke up those powerful mules
we start out on the road
to the source of his race

no better team to get us there
than yours that took the prize
at Olympia

          I open the praise gates
must make
Pitana today
          by the ford at Eurotas
with time to spare

             Pitana
who slept with the sea-god
          and bore him a daughter
Evadna
      hair, violet, dark

nine months
she hid the growing mound in the folds of her dress
(a virgin still)
           then slaves
carried the child
to the Arkadian king for keeping

Evadna grew
to beauty there

the first she knew of love was in
Apollo's arms
            with child by the god, she tried
to hide it

            but the king had eyes
travelled to Delphi
to ask the oracle's truth

rage clenched like a stone

Evadna
took off her belt
            purple studded with gold
put down
her silver jug, lay
            in the shadow of a bush
to bear her child

Apollo sent
the goddess of birth
                        and the destinies

Iamos
born of her pain
came crying into the light

grief
she must leave him there
helpless on his bed of leaves

two grey-eyed snakes
divine nurses
fed him the innocent venom of bees

The king rode back from Delphi
the stony road

"Where is this child of Evadna's…
greatest of prophets…
immortal his race…"

but they had heard nothing
                    seen nothing
and the child
                    five days old
                                        (lay
in a wilderness of reeds
among violets
                    yellow and dark, their light
                                        painting his limbs)
and his mother
whispered his name

"Iamos … immortal"

"...Iamos"

time came
to pluck the first petal of youth

went down to the river Alpheos
                    wading midstream
cried to the lord Poseidon
                    his mother's father
and to his father Apollo
                    of Delos, the archer
cried
for his birthright a king
                    under the clear night sky
and Apollo
came as his echo

                    "My son
it is time to leave this place

follow my voice   it will guide you"

                    ...Kronion
sheer cliff
where
Apollo gave his son
a double gift of prophecy

to hear a voice that never lies
to know, when Herakles comes

scion of the great oak
to found the games and festival
                    of Olympia
Iamos will build
an oracle on the highest altar of Zeus

success since then
wealth
        for Iamos' race
throughout
the mainland and the islands

such virtues and gifts
the eye of Greece their
                  permanent sun and moon
their straight path

it is the act proves the man
            there is also envy

the petty who scowl
as the team drives past the last post
                as victory
lights
the winner's face

                    Hagesias

if it is true

that your mother's race

                    in the foothills of Kyllana

have sacrificed and prayed

to Hermes

                    herald of gods

master of games and lord protector

                    of the Arkadians

then

it is he and father Zeus

whose radiance

…that high, clear note
        singing of bees on my tongue

                …or birds

I am drawn
        I come
                …on the songstream
Metopa
among flowers
                my mother's mother
Metopa
vhose child was Theba
                Thebes, her cool streams
nourishing this song
of fighting men

Aineas, master of singers
throw your whole choir into song
                    for the maiden Hera
sing my poem–
drown out the old insult
                    "Boiotian pigs"
You are my messenger
cipher-stick
          my song unwinding
music and words
mingling in the great bowl of sound

Tell them: remember Syracuse
and the Isle of Quails
                where Hieron rules so
justly, applying his whole mind
          observing the rites of Demeter
at blood gold harvest
                    Persephona too
and white horses unmelting
                    out of the earth
bringing her back
and Zeus, lord of Aitna

the soft voice of the harp
knows Hieron
and the dancing

may he shine
with future suns

his deep heart hear
this victory choir for Hagesias
and be proud

the song
coming from home
            coming home

from a walled city in Arkadia
a land of grazing sheep

on a stormy night
wise ship/
                two anchors
Arkadia
Syracuse

Zeus
bring them fame and contentment

Poseidon
lord of earth's waters
            Amphitrita by you

her nape
bent over the gold spindle

grant them a quick
                and flawless passage

make the seed of my songs ripen
make them be flowers

About the Translator

David Wevill was born a Canadian in Yokohama, Japan, where his family had been living for two generations, in 1935. The family left for Canada before the outbreak of World War II. Wevill grew up in Canada and moved to England during the 1950s, read History and English at Caius College, Cambridge, and gained a reputation as a leading young poet in the 1960s. He lived in London, where he was associated with The Group, a gathering of young poets who met frequently to discuss their work. He moved to Texas in the late 1960s, where he co-edited *Delos: A Journal on and of Translation* and taught at the University of Texas at Austin until his retirement. His poetry was first showcased in the Penguin Modern Poets series and has since been awarded with an Arts Council Book Prize, the Richard Hillary Prize, two Arts Council Poetry Bursaries, an E.C. Gregory Trust Award, and a Guggenheim Fellowship. His work has appeared in numerous publications, including *The New York Times, The New Yorker, Poetry* (Chicago), *Harper's, The Listener, The Observer, The Spectator,* and on the BBC. In 2022 his *Collected Poems* were published by Shearsman Books in two volumes. David Wevill lives in Austin, Texas.